Using the Standards
Algebra

Grade 1

by
Terry Huston

Published by Instructional Fair
an imprint of
Frank Schaffer Publications®

Instructional Fair

Author: Terry Huston
Editor: Karen Thompson

Frank Schaffer Publications®

Instructional Fair is an imprint of Frank Schaffer Publications.

Send all inquiries to:
Frank Schaffer Publications
3195 Wilson Drive NW
Grand Rapids, Michigan 49534

Using the Standards: Algebra—grade 1

ISBN: 0-7424-2881-8

3 4 5 6 7 8 9 10 PAT 09 08 07 06

Table of Contents

Published by Instructional Fair. Copyright protected.   0-7424-2881-8 *Using the Standards—Algebra*

Introduction

For those people who had a bad experience with algebra in high school or junior high school, the very idea of teaching algebra in first grade must seem downright insane. While adults may look on algebra as finding *x* or factoring equations, children have no such preconceived notions.

We invite skeptics to roam through this book. There are no linear equations, no parabolic graphs, and no exponential expressions. It's all "normal" math—with one exception. Instead of expecting children to learn addition facts by rote, we show them the whys and wherefores. When do you add? How can we all speak the same language of mathematics? Which numbers can form patterns? Where do these patterns lead us? Children are curious and willing to investigate these aspects of math.

This book has been designed around the National Council of Teachers of Mathematics standards for Algebra. It is designed to complement any mathematics program. You may choose to use the pages as they coordinate with your classroom activities. For easy reference, they are organized in four major categories: Patterns and Functions, Situations and Structures, Models, and Changes in Context.

Chapter 1, **Patterns and Functions**, progresses from simple sorting exercises to more complex sorting and ordering. Children will learn to recognize attributes of objects—shape, color, size, use, and magnitude. Once they have established good recognition skills, they are ready to order the objects, and then to recognize, extend, and create patterns. Both repeating patterns and growing patterns are investigated.

In Chapter 2, **Situations and Structures**, children begin to use the symbols of mathematics. They learn that when we all use the same symbols, we can all understand exactly what is being "said." They begin moving from using pictures to using numbers as another step to learning the shorthand language of mathematics.

Chapter 2, **Models**, leads children to develop a method for putting all these symbols together in a coherent manner. They begin to translate simple real-life problems into the mathematics shorthand and learn to work with the numbers to solve problems. In many ways, the transferring of one pattern to another they did in Chapter 1 becomes translating words into numbers.

Chapter 4, **Changes in Context**, shows children how things in the world can change over time. Sometimes we can measure this change numerically. Did it get longer? How much longer? This also helps to integrate the symbolic notation of mathematics into their daily lives.

                    0-7424-2881-8 *Using the Standards—Algebra*

Introduction (cont.)

In accordance with the NCTM standards, each activity is linked to one or more of the five major process strands for mathematics:

Problem Solving   Communication   Reasoning and Proof

Representation   Connections

The main focus of the activity will be shown at the top of the page. You can also consult the NCTM Algebra Standards Correlation Chart on page 6 to see which content and process standards are found on each page.

Problem Solving asks for that extra brainwork. These kinds of problems are the sneaky sort. They do not ask children to come up with the same old answer, but to ponder on what is being asked and the best method for approach. Should I add or subtract? Maybe I should add first, then subtract. Activities marked as Problem Solving assume the child has the background, skills, and tools to perform the required math but must think about the solving process creatively.

Communication can vary from explaining clearly how you solved a problem to writing number sentences that any other child can understand. Children are asked to give explanations to their teacher, their class, and their peers. Successful communication results in comprehension by others. At the same time, it requires organized thought. Children who are challenged to tell about what they were thinking or how they went about solving a problem are also learning to think for themselves in a logical manner.

Representations can be just about any means of written communication. Some children will excel at drawing pictures, while others may become more adept at using mathematical symbols. Activities give each child a chance to express ideas through various representations.

Reasoning and Proof meshes with Problem Solving and Communication. Now when children are asked to explain their thinking, they have the tools with which to logically defend their decisions. Not only can they say that "seven is greater than five" but they can use physical or mathematical means to justify their statements.

Connections give us a reason and a justification for learning about mathematics. "Which turtle has more toes?" leads to "Which detergent is the better buy?" A few more steps and we arrive at "Which rocket fuel is more powerful?" and "Which stock shows a better return on investment?" Algebra is not just equations with x and y. Algebra is learning to think clearly and logically about the world in which we live. Students will also see connections between Algebra and other branches of mathematics, such as Geometry or Data Analysis.

     0-7424-2881-8 *Using the Standards—Algebra*

NCTM Algebra Standards Correlation Chart

	Problem Solving	Reasoning and Proof	Communication	Connections	Representation
Patterns and Functions					
sort, classify, and order objects	11, 12, 15, 17, 18, 20, 41	10, 19, 21, 22	9, 11, 12, 16, 17, 22	9, 10	11, 13, 14, 16, 40
recognize, describe, and extend patterns	24, 27, 28, 29	24, 26, 31, 33	26, 29, 32	25, 30, 32, 33	23, 25, 27, 30, 34
analyze repeating and growing patterns	37	35, 39, 43	35, 36, 39, 43	38	35, 36, 39, 42
Situations and Structures					
illustrate principles and properties of operations	54	48, 49, 51, 52, 54	46, 47, 49, 52	47, 48, 51, 53, 55, 78	46, 47, 51, 54, 55
symbolic notations	50, 56, 58, 59, 60, 61		47, 56, 58, 59, 60, 66	47, 53, 55, 63, 64, 65, 66, 67	47, 55, 57, 59, 60, 61, 62, 63, 64, 65, 66, 67
Models					
model addition and subtraction of whole numbers	72, 73, 74, 75, 76, 77, 79, 80, 81	74, 75, 77	76, 79, 81	63, 65, 67, 72, 73, 78, 79	63, 65, 67, 70, 71, 80, 81
Changes in Context					
describe qualitive change	87	84, 85, 89	84, 85, 86, 88, 90	87, 90, 91, 92, 93, 94	86, 88
describe quantitive change	97, 99, 101, 102, 103, 104, 105, 106	98, 100	96, 102, 106	95, 96, 100	95, 96, 97, 101, 102, 105, 106

*The pretest, posttest, Create Your Own Problems, and Check Your Skills pages are not included on this chart, but contain a representative sampling of the process standards.

0-7424-2881-8 *Using the Standards—Algebra*

Pretest

1. Find the pattern. Draw the next three shapes in the pattern.

2. Find the pattern. Make the same pattern using colors.

1 1 2 5 1 1 2 5 1 1 2 5

3. Write + or − to make each sentence true.

a. 6 ◯ 2 = 4   **d.** 10 ◯ 5 = 5

b. 3 ◯ 4 = 7   **e.** 6 ◯ 3 = 9

c. 9 ◯ 5 = 4   **f.** 5 ◯ 7 = 12

4. Write >, <, or =.

a. 5 ◯ 9   **d.** 8 ◯ 7

b. 10 ◯ 10   **e.** 6 ◯ 3

c. 2 ◯ 8   **f.** 3 ◯ 3

7

Pretest (cont.)

5. Write an addition or subtraction sentence to solve each problem.

a. Seven princesses went to a ball. Four of the princesses were wearing sneakers. How many princesses were not wearing sneakers? _____

b. Eight frogs were playing basketball. Two more frogs came to play. How many frogs were playing basketball altogether? _____

c. Two ponies were in the park playing horseshoes. Five ponies were swimming in the park. How many ponies in all were in the park? _____

6. Circle the things that have changed.

7. Read the clues and circle the mystery numbers.

a. I am > 3. I am < 6. What numbers could I be?

1 2 3 4 5 6 7 8 9 10 11 12 13 14 15

b. I am > 9. I am < 14. What numbers could I be?

1 2 3 4 5 6 7 8 9 10 11 12 13 14 15

8

Name _____ Date _____

What's the Same?

Directions: Tell how the shapes in each group are alike. Draw two more shapes that belong in each group.

1.

2.

3.

THINK

How are the shapes in each group different from the shapes in the other groups? How could you sort the shapes in a different way?

0-7424-2881-8 *Using the Standards—Algebra*

Name _____ Date _____

The Shape of Things

Directions: Circle all the shapes that have four corners and four sides.

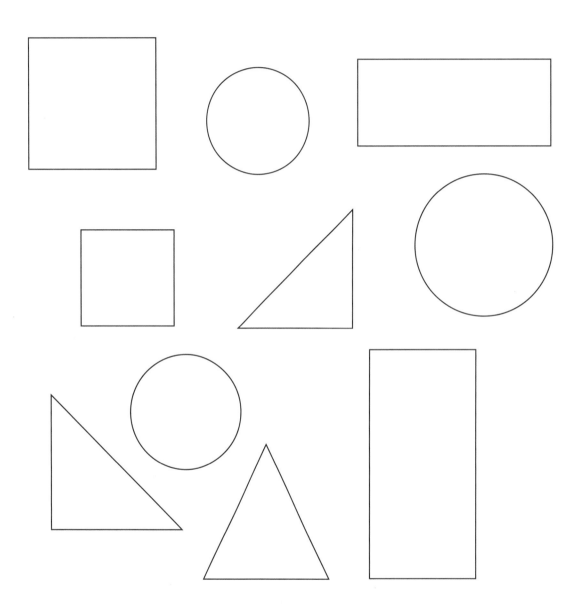

DO MORE

Use red and blue crayons to color all the shapes. Cut out the shapes and sort the shapes by their color. How else could you sort the shapes?

0-7424-2881-8 *Using the Standards—Algebra*

Name _____ Date _____

Sort, Sort, Sort!

Directions: Cut out these boxes. Sort the shapes in three different ways.

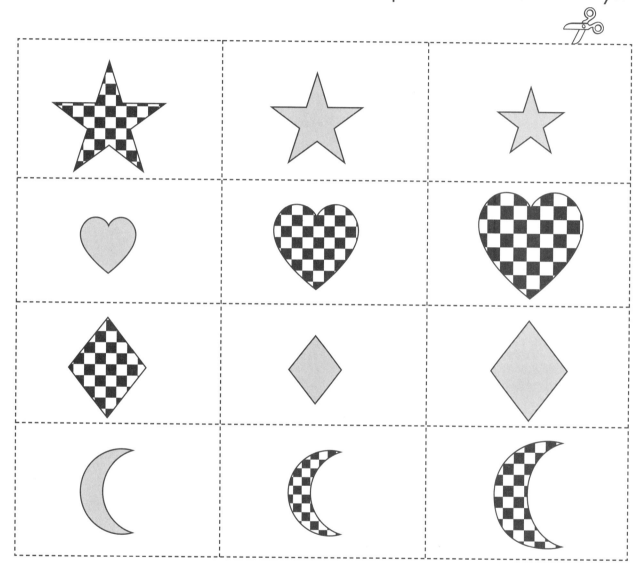

Choose your favorite way you sorted the shapes. Paste the shapes on a piece of paper to show this way. Show your paper to your class. Explain how you sorted the shapes.

DO MORE

How many different ways could you sort the shapes?

0-7424-2881-8 *Using the Standards—Algebra*

Name _____ Date _____

The Key to My Heart

Directions: Which one is my heart? Listen to the clues.

My heart is not a small heart. Cross out all the small hearts.

My heart is not a striped heart. Cross out all the striped hearts.

My heart is not upside down. Cross out all the upside-down hearts.

Color my heart red.

DO MORE

Describe how you could sort all the hearts on the page.

0-7424-2881-8 *Using the Standards—Algebra*

Name _____ Date _____

Monster Mittens

Directions: Match each monster with the correct number of mittens it will need this winter.

1.    6

2.    4

3.    5

4.    7

5.   3

DO MORE

Draw your own monster. Write the number of mittens it will need. Have a friend draw the correct number of mittens.

13

Published by Instructional Fair. Copyright protected.

Name _____ Date _____

In Style

Directions: Draw lines to show a matching dress, hat, and purse for each person. You decide which outfit would look best on each person.

DO MORE

Use a different color. Draw lines to show outfits where nothing matches.

0-7424-2881-8 *Using the Standards—Algebra*

Name _____ Date _____

In Full Bloom

Directions: Look at the flowers. Circle two flowers if they are next to each other and have the same number of petals. Look up and down, left and right.

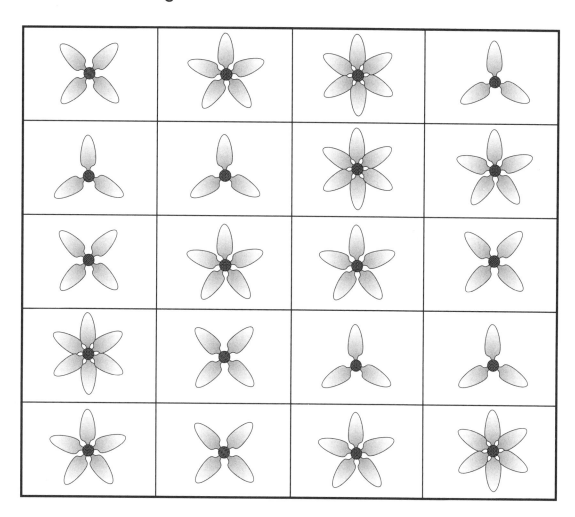

How many pairs of matching flowers did you find? _____

DO MORE

Use a red crayon to circle the flowers with 4 petals.
Use an orange crayon to circle the flowers with 5 petals.

0-7424-2881-8 *Using the Standards—Algebra*

Name _____ Date _____

Train of Thought

First

Directions: Follow each direction below.

1. Color the third car in the train blue.

2. Mark an X on the eighth car in the train.

3. Circle the sixth car in the train.

4. Color the fourth car yellow.

DO MORE

Use 9 cubes of one color and 1 cube of a different color. Make a cube train by putting all the cubes together. Tell a friend the position of the different-colored cube. Have your friend make the train.

Published by Instructional Fair. Copyright protected.   0-7424-2881-8 *Using the Standards—Algebra*

Name _____ Date _____

A Sunny Day in Beartown

Directions: Draw a circle around all the bears that are holding umbrellas.
Color the small bears with sunglasses brown.

THINK

Did you color all the small bears? Why or why not? Describe the bears
you did not circle or color.

0-7424-2881-8 *Using the Standards—Algebra*

Patterns and Functions

Name _____ Date _____

Yummy, Yummy

Directions: Circle the things that are cold.
Mark an X on the things you can drink.

THINK

What do the things you did not circle have in common? What do the things you did not mark with an X have in common? What do all the things on the page have in common?

18

0-7424-2881-8 *Using the Standards—Algebra*

Name _____ Date _____

Button Up!

Directions: Number the shirts in order from the one with the fewest buttons to the one with the most buttons.

1.

_____
- - - - - - - - - - - -
_____

2.

_____
- - - - - - - - - - - -
_____

3.

_____
- - - - - - - - - - - -
_____

DO MORE

Draw a shirt with 5 buttons. If this shirt were added to each group of shirts, how would the order change?

19

0-7424-2881-8 *Using the Standards—Algebra*

Name _____ Date _____

Read Any Good Books Lately?

1. Write numbers to show the order of the books from the smallest to the largest.

_____

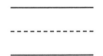
_____

World Atlas
_____

_____

_____

2. Write numbers to show the order of the books from the largest to smallest.

_____

_____

_____

_____

_____

DO MORE

Find 4 books in your classroom or library. Put them in order from smallest to largest.

0-7424-2881-8 *Using the Standards—Algebra*

Name _____ Date _____

Scrambled Stories

Directions: Number the pictures in the order that they happened.

1.

_____ _____ _____

2.

_____ _____ _____

3.

_____ _____ _____

DO MORE

Think of three things you did in the summer.
Draw them in the order that they happened.

0-7424-2881-8 *Using the Standards—Algebra*

Name _____ Date _____

New Girl in Town

Directions: Look at the pictures.
Number the events in the order they happened.

a.

_____
- - - - - - - -
_____

b.

_____
- - - - - - - -
_____

c.

_____
- - - - - - - -
_____

d.

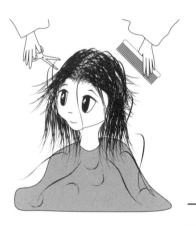

_____
- - - - - - - -
_____

THINK

Explain how you know the correct order of the events.

0-7424-2881-8 *Using the Standards—Algebra*

Name _____ Date _____

One, Two, Three

Directions: Count by 3s. Color the squares with these numbers pink. Tell what pattern you see.

1	2	3	4	5	6	7	8	9	10
11	12	13	14	15	16	17	18	19	20
21	22	23	24	25	26	27	28	29	30
31	32	33	34	35	36	37	38	39	40
41	42	43	44	45	46	47	48	49	50
51	52	53	54	55	56	57	58	59	60
61	62	63	64	65	66	67	68	69	70

Now count by 3s to connect the dots.
Use the number chart to help you.

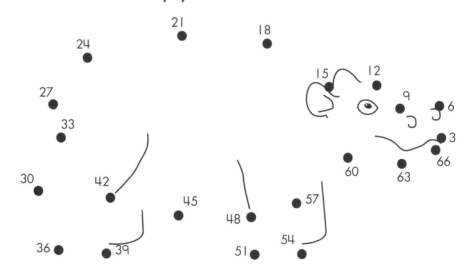

DO MORE

Count by 4s. Use a red crayon to circle each number in the chart as you count. Tell what pattern you see.

0-7424-2881-8 *Using the Standards—Algebra*

Name _____ Date _____

Again and Again and Again

Directions: Find the shape pattern in each row.
Draw the next shape in each pattern.

1.

◯◯△△◯◯△△◯◯△

2.

▢◯△△▢◯△△▢◯△△▢◯△

3.

♡♡▢◯♡♡▢◯♡♡▢

4.

☆△♡△☆△♡△☆△♡△

THINK

For each pattern, what is the group of shapes that is repeated? Circle one of the groups in each pattern.

0-7424-2881-8 *Using the Standards—Algebra*

Name _____ Date _____

Lions and Tigers and Bears

Directions: Look at the patterns of animals. Circle the animal that comes next in each pattern.

DO MORE

What does a cow sound like? What does a lion sound like? Use these sounds to make a sound pattern.

0-7424-2881-8 *Using the Standards—Algebra*

Name _____ Date _____

What's Missing Here?

Directions: Find the pattern in each row. Draw the fruit that is missing in each pattern.

1.   ☐

2.   ☐

3.  ☐

4.   ☐

5. ☐

DO MORE

Choose one pattern. Tell a friend which three objects would come next.

0-7424-2881-8 *Using the Standards—Algebra*

Pattern Synonyms

Directions: These two patterns are the same.
Study the pattern. Then follow the directions.

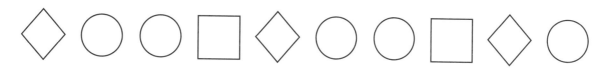

$$3 \quad 4 \quad 4 \quad 7 \quad 3 \quad 4 \quad 4 \quad 7 \quad 3 \quad 4$$

1. Use colors to show the same pattern.

2. Make two new patterns that are the same.
Use a number pattern and a color pattern.

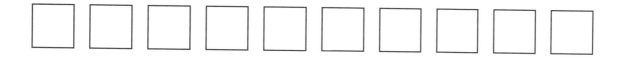

DO MORE

Make a movement pattern.
Have a friend make a sound pattern that is the same.

27

0-7424-2881-8 *Using the Standards—Algebra*

Name _____ Date _____

Little Red Riding Hood's Hoods

Directions: Little Red Riding Hood has 7 hoods, one for each day of the week. She keeps track of her hoods by looking at the shape pattern. Continue the pattern on the next three hoods.

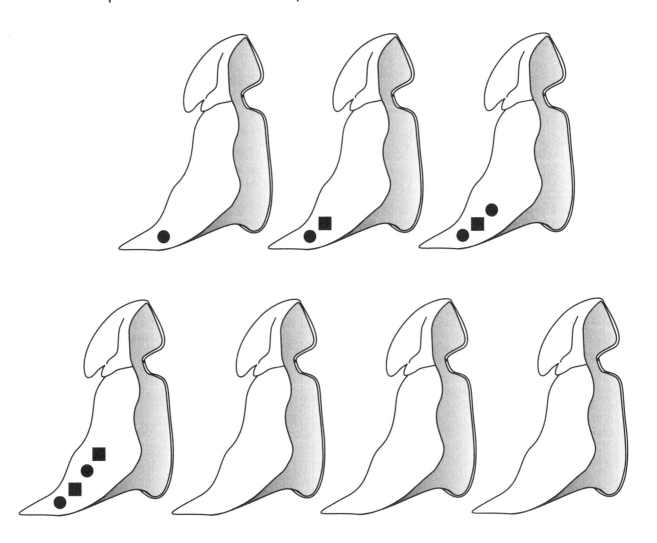

DO MORE

Write a number pattern under each hood above to match the shape pattern.

0-7424-2881-8 *Using the Standards—Algebra*

Name _____ Date _____

Unlock the Door

Directions: The part of the pattern that repeats will open one of the
doors. Find and circle the part of the pattern that repeats.
Match the pattern to the correct door.

1. 1 2 2 3 1 2 2 3 1 2

2. 2 1 2 3 2 1 2 3 2 1

3. 1 1 3 2 1 1 3 2 1 1

4. 3 3 1 2 3 3 1 2 3 3

5. 1 3 2 1 1 3 2 1 1 3

| 2123 |
| 1223 |
| 3312 |
| 1321 |
| 1132 |

DO MORE

Make up your own number pattern. Tell what part of the pattern repeats.

0-7424-2881-8 *Using the Standards—Algebra*

Name _____ Date _____

Covering Patterns

Directions: You can use some shapes to completely cover an area. Draw more of each covering shape pattern.

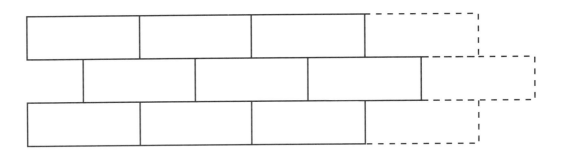

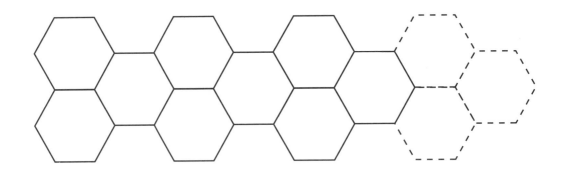

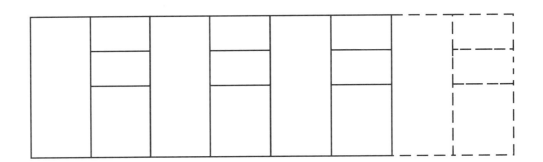

DO MORE

Color each covering pattern so that it shows a color pattern, too.

0-7424-2881-8 *Using the Standards—Algebra*

Name _____ Date _____

Pretend Patterns

Directions: In the rows that show patterns, circle the part of the pattern that repeats. Write **no pattern** on the rows that have no pattern.

1. 8 3 8 9 8 3 8 9 8 3 8 9 8 3 8 9

_____

2. 1 4 1 5 9 2 6 5 3 5 9 7 4 2 9 6

_____

3. H J K P H J K P H J K P H J K

_____

4.

_____

5.

_____

THINK

How could you prove to a friend that there is no pattern in a row you marked?

0-7424-2881-8 *Using the Standards—Algebra*

Name _____ Date _____

Simon Says

Directions: Read each direction and do what Simon says.

1	2	3						9	
				16					
	23								
			35						
	42								

1. Simon says to fill in the missing numbers in the chart.

2. Simon says circle the number that is one square after 18.

3. Simon says circle the number that is one square before 32.

4. Simon says circle the number that is two squares after 27.

5. Simon says circle the number that is two squares before 15.

6. Simon says circle the number that is four squares after 44.

7. Simon says circle the number that is three squares before 39.

8. Simon says circle the number that is five squares after 18.

DO MORE

Make up some Simon says directions for the number chart.
Have a friend find the correct numbers.

0-7424-2881-8 *Using the Standards—Algebra*

Name _____ Date _____

Copycat

Directions: The part of the pattern that repeats is shown. Draw the pattern.

1. □ □ ○ △

2. 5 7 0 7

3. 9 9 3 5

4. S P H T

5. △ ○ □ ○

Which pairs of patterns are the same? _____

THINK

How could you check your pattern to see if it is drawn correctly?
Use one of the patterns to show how.

0-7424-2881-8 *Using the Standards—Algebra*

Name _____ Date _____

Growing Up

Directions: Look at each pattern to see how it grows.
Draw what comes next.

1.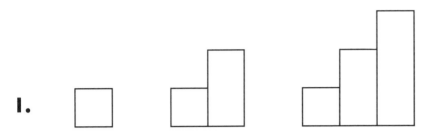

2.

3.

THINK

Look at the pattern for Problem 3. Tell how many rectangles are in the bottom row. Can you tell how many rectangles would be in the tenth row of the pattern?

34

0-7424-2881-8 *Using the Standards—Algebra*

Name _____ Date _____

Can I Have Your Number?

Directions: These patterns are growing patterns. The lines show the parts of the pattern. Look at the parts and find the rule for each pattern. Write the next part.

1.

5 3 | 5 3 3 | 5 3 3 3 |

2.

8 1 | 8 8 1 1 |

3.

7 4 7 | 7 4 4 7 |

DO MORE

Explain the rule for each pattern.

0-7424-2881-8 *Using the Standards—Algebra*

Name _____ Date _____

The Same, But Different

Directions: Look at this growing pattern. Make the same pattern three different ways. Use shapes, colors, and different numbers.

| 1 | 1 | 2 | 1 | 2 | 3 | 1 | 2 | 3 | 4 |

_____

Shapes

_____

Colors

_____

Numbers

THINK

What is the rule for this pattern? Explain how you made the same pattern using shapes, colors, and different numbers.

0-7424-2881-8 *Using the Standards—Algebra*

Name _____ Date _____

Petal Patterns

Directions: Use a red crayon and a yellow crayon. Color the six flowers in six different ways. Color each petal one color. All the petals must be colored.

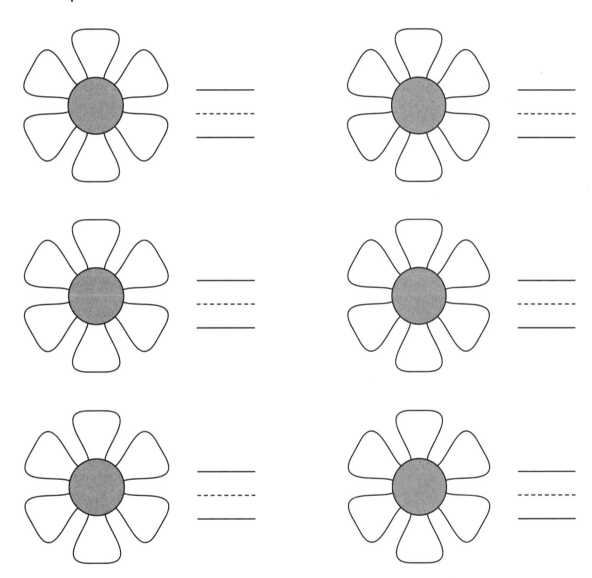

DO MORE

Number the flowers in order so the red petals show a growing pattern.

Published by Instructional Fair. Copyright protected.

0-7424-2881-8 *Using the Standards—Algebra*

Name _____ Date _____

Growing Shapes

Directions: Look at the shapes and see how they show a growing
pattern. Count the number of squares in each square.
Write the number.

1.

Number of Squares

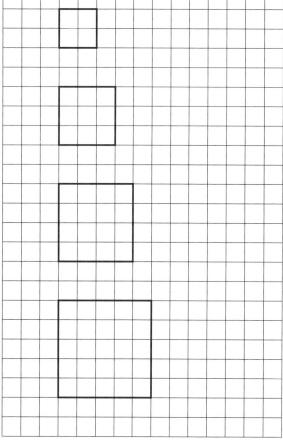

_____

_____

2.

_____

_____

3.

_____

_____

4.

_____

_____

Look at the numbers in order. Can you find a growing pattern?

DO MORE

Draw the next shape in the pattern and count the sides and the squares.
Does this shape follow the pattern?

 0-7424-2881-8 *Using the Standards—Algebra*

Name _____ Date _____

A Real Fashion Statement

Directions: Look at each pattern. Use three different colors that you like. Color the scarf in the same pattern.

1.

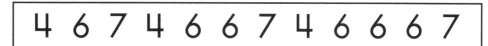

4 6 7 4 6 6 7 4 6 6 6 7

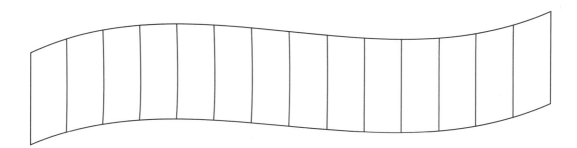

2.

5 9 2 5 9 2 5 9 2 5 9 2

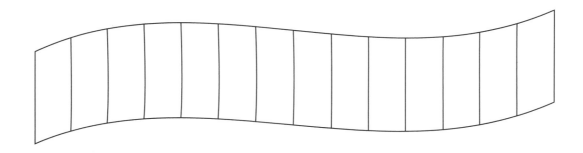

THINK

Look at each pattern. Tell whether it is a repeating pattern or a growing pattern. Explain how you know.

0-7424-2881-8 *Using the Standards—Algebra*

Name _____ Date _____

Secret Code

Directions: Some secret codes use the numbers of the letters of the alphabet. Number the letters in order.

A	B	C	D	E	F
1	2				

G	H	I	J	K	L

M	N	O	P	Q	R

S	T	U	V	W	X

Y	Z

Secret Code

0-7424-2881-8 *Using the Standards—Algebra*

Name _____ Date _____

Secret Code (cont.)

Directions: Find the letter for each number on page 40 to unlock the riddle and the answer.

____	____	____	____			
23	8	1	20			

____	____	____	____	____	____	____
3	12	15	20	8	5	19

____	____	____	____		____	
4	15	5	19		1	

____	____	____	____	____
8	15	21	19	5

?

____	____	____	____
23	5	1	18

____	____	____	____	____	____	____
1	4	4	18	5	19	19

DO MORE

Write three words using the code key.
Have a friend unlock your code.

0-7424-2881-8 *Using the Standards—Algebra*

Name _____ Date _____

Half Again

Directions: This growing pattern shows a square cut in half, and then cut in half again. Look at the pattern. Practice folding a scrap piece of paper. Then draw the next two parts of the pattern.

DO MORE

Do you think if you started with a larger square you could extend the pattern? Try it.

0-7424-2881-8 *Using the Standards—Algebra*

Name _____ Date _____

How Does Your Garden Grow?

Directions: Look at each pattern. Circle R if it is a repeating pattern. Circle G if it is a growing pattern.

1.

R

G

_____

2.

R

G

_____

3.

R

G

_____

4.

R

G

_____

5.

R

G

DO MORE

Choose one repeating pattern. Explain how you decided it was a repeating pattern. Then do the same for one of the growing patterns.

0-7424-2881-8 *Using the Standards—Algebra*

Name _____ Date _____

Create Your Own Problems

Directions: Use the boxes below to make two problems about patterns. Draw one repeating pattern and one growing pattern.

0-7424-2881-8 *Using the Standards—Algebra*

Name _____ Date _____

Check Your Skills

1. Circle all the large hearts with stripes.

2. Number the flowers in order from smallest to largest.

_____   _____   _____   _____

- - - - - - -   - - - - - - -   - - - - - - -   - - - - - - -

_____   _____   _____   _____

3. Circle the part of each pattern that repeats.

1   5   3   1   5   3   1   5   3

O   F   F   O   F   F   O   F   F

4. Draw the rest of the pattern.

     0-7424-2881-8 *Using the Standards—Algebra*

Name _____ Date _____

Equal Rights–and Lefts

Directions: Look at the blocks on the scale.
Draw blocks to make the scale balance.

1.

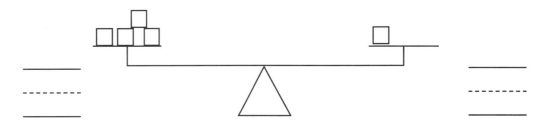

_____   _____
- - - - - -   - - - - - -

2.

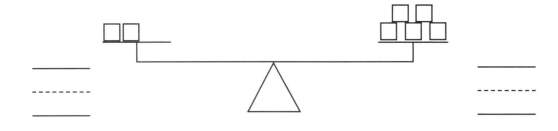

_____   _____
- - - - - -   - - - - - -

3.

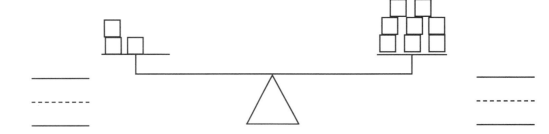

- - - - - -   - - - - - -

Write the number of blocks on each side of the scale now.

THINK

How do you know your scales are balanced?

     0-7424-2881-8 *Using the Standards—Algebra*

Name _____ Date _____

Make It Equal

Directions: Circle the correct number of fish to make each statement true.

1.

$9 =$

2.

$7 =$

3.

$10 =$

4.

$12 =$

DO MORE

What does the equal sign tell you about the two things it connects?

0-7424-2881-8 *Using the Standards—Algebra*

Name _____ Date _____

Button, Button

Directions: Count the number of buttons in each group.
Circle **more** or **less** to make the sentence true.

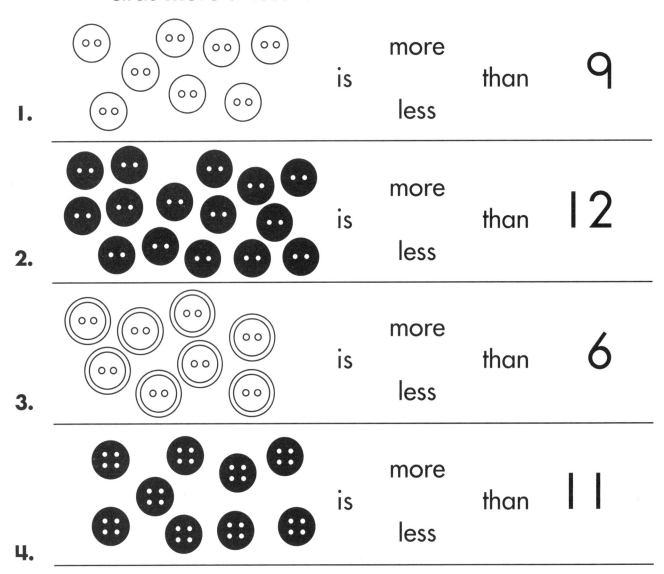

1.   more
   is   than   9
      less

2.   more
   is   than   12
      less

3.   more
   is   than   6
      less

4.   more
   is   than   11
      less

DO MORE

Play with a friend, using counters and number cards. Put the number cards facedown on the table. One friend counts out 1 to 10 counters. The other draws a card from the pile. The one with the greater number wins. Put the card and the counters back, trade places, and play again.

0-7424-2881-8 *Using the Standards—Algebra*

Name _____ Date _____

More Than One Answer

Directions: Write a number that makes each sentence true. Then draw the dots on the domino.

1. [box] _____ / ------- / _____   is less than 7 [domino]

2. [box] _____ / ------- / _____   is more than 5 [domino]

3. [box] _____ / ------- / _____   is less than 9 [domino]

4. [box] _____ / ------- / _____   is more than 8 [domino]

THINK

Compare your answers with a friend. Are the answers the same?
Can you both be correct? Explain why or why not.

0-7424-2881-8 *Using the Standards—Algebra*

Name _____ Date _____

Solve the Mystery

Directions: Read the clues for each problem.
Circle all the numbers that solve the mystery.

1. I am > 4. I am < 7. What numbers could I be?

1	2	3	4	5	6	7	8	9	10	11	12	13	14	15

2. I am > 8. I am < 13. What numbers could I be?

1	2	3	4	5	6	7	8	9	10	11	12	13	14	15

3. I am > 1. I am < 6. What numbers could I be?

1	2	3	4	5	6	7	8	9	10	11	12	13	14	15

4. I am > 6. I am < 14. What numbers could I be?

1	2	3	4	5	6	7	8	9	10	11	12	13	14	15

DO MORE

Make up your own clues about some numbers. Trade clues with a friend and find the mystery numbers.

0-7424-2881-8 *Using the Standards—Algebra*

Name _____ Date _____

Thanks for Nothing!

Directions: Count the dimes in each group. Solve the problem. Draw a group of dimes to show each answer.

1.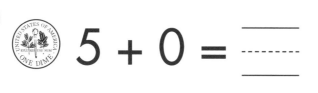

$5 + 0 = $ _____

2.

$9 + 0 = $ _____

3.

$7 - 0 = $ _____

4.

$4 - 0 = $ _____

THINK

Explain how adding or subtracting 0 changes a number.

0-7424-2881-8 *Using the Standards—Algebra*

Name _____ Date _____

What's the Story?

Directions: Read each story. Decide if you would add or subtract to find the answer. Circle the correct operation.

1. You have 7 keys. 2 keys fall off the chain.

add   **subtract**

2. You have 12 blue chickens. You get 4 more blue chickens for your birthday.

add   **subtract**

3. You have 9 turtles. Three of the turtles went for a swim.

add   **subtract**

4. You have 11 tennis trophies. You win 3 more trophies.

add   **subtract**

5. You have 10 light bulbs. Two of the light bulbs break.

add   **subtract**

DO MORE

Make up an addition story and a subtraction story. Tell the stories to a friend and have them decide whether to add or subtract.

     0-7424-2881-8 *Using the Standards—Algebra*

Name _____ Date _____

Touchdown!

Directions: Play this game with a friend. Roll two number cubes.

If the numbers you roll add to < 5, move 10 yards.

If the numbers you roll add to = 6, move 20 yards.

If the numbers you roll add to = 7, move 30 yards.

If the numbers you roll add to > 7, move 40 yards.

The first player to score 3 touchdowns wins.

yards

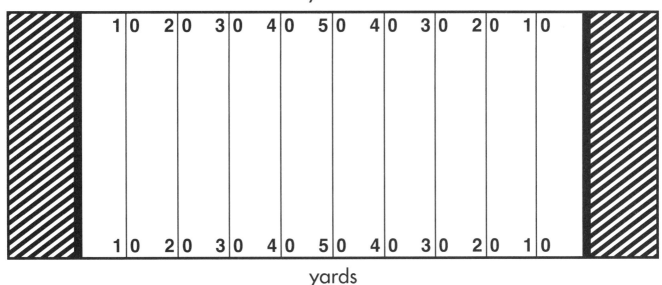

yards

DO MORE

Play again. Make up your own number rules.
Explain your rules to your class.

Published by Instructional Fair. Copyright protected.

0-7424-2881-8 *Using the Standards—Algebra*

Name _____ Date _____

You Be the Teacher

Directions: Your students were told to draw enough shapes to make ten. Are the answers on their papers correct? If the answer is wrong, draw or cross out shapes to make the answer correct.

1.

2.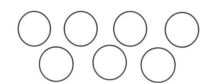

3.

4.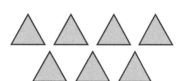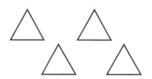

DO MORE

Find other ways to make ten. Use counters or drawings to show these other ways.

0-7424-2881-8 *Using the Standards—Algebra*

Name _____ Date _____

It's Puzzling

Directions: Read each number sentence. Draw lines to match the ones that use the same numbers.

1. $7 + 4 = 11$
2. $3 + 5 = 8$
3. $6 + 3 = 9$
4. $2 + 5 = 7$
5. $4 + 1 = 5$
6. $9 + 1 = 10$
7. $4 + 8 = 12$
8. $5 + 4 = 9$

a. $5 + 2 = 7$
b. $8 + 4 = 12$
c. $1 + 4 = 5$
d. $4 + 7 = 11$
e. $4 + 5 = 9$
f. $3 + 6 = 9$
g. $1 + 9 = 10$
h. $5 + 3 = 8$

THINK

What do you notice about the number sentences that match?

0-7424-2881-8 *Using the Standards—Algebra*

Name _____ Date _____

Oops!

Directions: Someone spilled milk on this paper. What number is covered by the spill? Use counters to help you find the missing number.

I. $4 +$ 〈 〉 $= 9$ The missing number is _____

2. $2 +$ 〈 〉 $= 10$ The missing number is _____

3. $6 +$ 〈 〉 $= 11$ The missing number is _____

4. $8 +$ 〈 〉 $= 12$ The missing number is _____

5. $3 +$ 〈 〉 $= 10$ The missing number is _____

DO MORE

Choose one problem. Explain to a friend how you found the missing number.

0-7424-2881-8 *Using the Standards—Algebra*

Name _____ Date _____

Mixed Signals

Directions: Compare the two numbers and color the correct sign.

1.

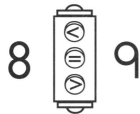

2.

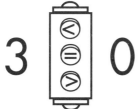

3.

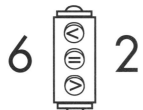

4.

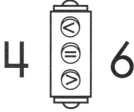

5.

5 < = > 5

6.

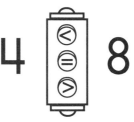

DO MORE

Play with a friend. Choose two number cards. Your friend must choose the correct sign to show how the numbers compare. Trade places and play again.

 0-7424-2881-8 *Using the Standards—Algebra*

Name _____ Date _____

Signs of the Times

Directions: Write + to show addition. Write − to show subtraction.
Write + or − in the circle to make each number sentence true.

1. 9 ◯ 3 = 12

2. 5 ◯ 4 = 9

3. 11 ◯ 6 = 5

4. 3 ◯ 3 = 0

5. 2 ◯ 6 = 8

THINK

Choose one of the problems. Explain how you decided whether to use the plus sign or the minus sign.

0-7424-2881-8 *Using the Standards—Algebra*

Name _____ Date _____

Do It Yourself

Directions: Make up your own symbols for addition, subtraction, and equality. Use your symbols to complete each number sentence.

```
My Symbols

+          _____

−          _____

=          _____
```

1.

8 ◯ 3 ◯ 5

2.

2 ◯ 7 ◯ 9

3.

5 ◯ 6 ◯ 11

THINK

Do you think math is easier if everybody has their own symbols, or if we all use the same symbols? Explain.

0-7424-2881-8 *Using the Standards—Algebra*

Name _____ Date _____

A Rose By Any Other Name

All these are names for the number 5: **1 + 4   6 – 1   3 + 2**

Directions: Write two names for each number.

1. 7 _____

2. 12 _____

3. 6 _____

4. 10 _____

5. 3 _____

6. 8 _____

7. 11 _____

8. 9 _____

9. 4 _____

10. 2 _____

THINK

Compare your answers with those of a friend. Do you both have the same answers? Could you both have answers that are correct? Explain.

Name _____ Date _____

Treasure Hunt

Directions: Read the clues and find the stepping-stones with those answers. Color those stones to help you find the path to the treasure.

CLUES		
8 – 6	6 + 3	12 – 1
7 + 1	10 – 5	8 – 4
11 + 2	7 + 5	8 + 8

START

(2) (17) (6) (7) (19)

(14) (8) (20) (15) (21)

(10) (13) (9) (5) (24)

(23) (26) (22) (12) (25)

(18) (3) (11) (4) (16)

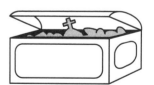

DO MORE

Make up your own clues for the same stepping-stones. Have a friend solve the puzzle using your clues.

0-7424-2881-8 *Using the Standards—Algebra*

Name _____ Date _____

It's a Jungle Out There

Directions: Cut out the pictures at the right. Paste the pictures in the correct column of the pictograph, starting at the bottom. Count the number of pictures in each column.

_____   _____   _____

- - - - - - -   - - - - - - -   - - - - - - -

_____   _____   _____

0-7424-2881-8 *Using the Standards—Algebra*

Name _____ Date _____

Reading Pictures

Directions: Read the pictograph and answer the questions. ☺ = 1 student

Vanilla	☺	☺	☺	☺	☺	☺	
Chocolate	☺	☺	☺	☺	☺	☺	☺
Strawberry	☺	☺	☺				
Peanut Butter							

1. How many students like vanilla ice cream?

_____

2. How many students like chocolate ice cream?

_____

3. How many students like strawberry and vanilla ice cream?

_____

4. How many students like chocolate and vanilla ice cream?

_____

5. How many more students like chocolate ice cream better than strawberry ice cream?

_____

DO MORE

Ask 10 friends if they like peanut-butter ice cream. Draw a face in the pictograph for each "yes" answer.

0-7424-2881-8 *Using the Standards—Algebra*

Name _____ Date _____

Best Graph, Bar None

Directions: Count the number of each kind of pet. Color one square for each pet. Start at the bottom of the graph and work up. Then count the number of each kind of pet.

_____   _____   _____

- - - - -   - - - - -   - - - - -

_____   _____   _____

THINK

How can you easily find the most popular kind of pet from the graph?

Published by Instructional Fair. Copyright protected.

0-7424-2881-8 *Using the Standards—Algebra*

Name _____ Date _____

Communicating

Directions: This bar graph shows how people communicate most often. Read the bar graph and answer the questions.

Telephone								
Mail								
E-mail								
Cell Phone								

1. How many people use a telephone? _____

2. How many people use e-mail? _____

3. How many people use mail and e-mail? _____

4. How many people use the telephone and e-mail? _____

5. How many more people use e-mail than mail? _____

DO MORE

Ask ten friends if they have used a cell phone.
Color one square for each "yes" answer.

Published by Instructional Fair. Copyright protected.
0-7424-2881-8 *Using the Standards—Algebra*

Name _____ Date _____

A New Way to Count

Directions: Count each kind of animal. Make one tally mark in the chart for each animal you count.

🦉	
🐬	
🐢	

THINK

Is it easier to look at the pictures or look at the tally chart to see if there are more owls than turtles?

0-7424-2881-8 *Using the Standards—Algebra*

Name _____ Date _____

Reading the Handwriting

Directions: Look at the tally chart. Use the tally chart to help answer the questions.

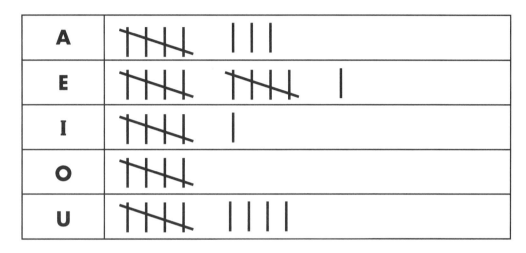

A	卌			
E	卌 卌	
I	卌	
O	卌
U	卌				

1. How many As are shown?

_____
- - - - - - -

2. How many Os are shown?

_____
_____
- - - - - - -

3. How many Es and Us are shown?

_____
_____
- - - - - - -

4. How many more Es than Is are shown?

_____
_____
- - - - - - -

5. How many Is and Us are shown?

_____
_____
- - - - - - -
_____

DO MORE

Make a tally chart to show how many boys and how many girls are in your class.

0-7424-2881-8 *Using the Standards—Algebra*

Name _____ Date _____

Create Your Own Problems

Directions: Use the graph to make up your own problem.

Think: Will you make a pictograph or a bar graph?

Think: What will you count?

Count the _____.

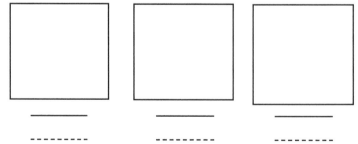

0-7424-2881-8 *Using the Standards—Algebra*

Check Your Skills

1. Draw blocks to make the scale balance.

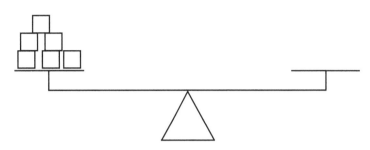

2. Write + or − to make each number sentence true.

a. 5 ◯ 6 = 11

b. 9 ◯ 2 = 7

c. 7 ◯ 2 = 5

d. 4 ◯ 6 = 10

3. Write > , <, or =

a. 8 ◯ 5

b. 6 ◯ 6

c. 10 ◯ 12

d. 7 ◯ 3

4. Circle all the number that could be the mystery number.

a. I am > 8. I am < 13. What numbers could I be?

1	2	3	4	5	6	7	8	9	10	11	12	13	14	15

b. I am > 2. I am < 7. What numbers could I be?

1	2	3	4	5	6	7	8	9	10	11	12	13	14	15

0-7424-2881-8 *Using the Standards—Algebra*

Name _____ Date _____

That Adds Up!

Directions: Write the addition sentence shown by the pictures.

1.

_____

2.

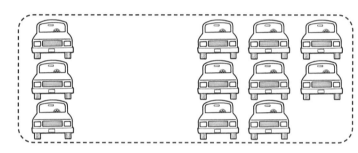

_____

3.

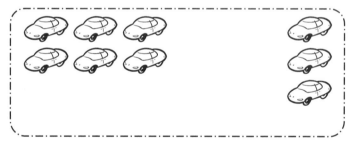

_____

4.

_____

DO MORE

Read each addition sentence aloud.

0-7424-2881-8 *Using the Standards—Algebra*

Name _____ Date _____

Less Than Before

Directions: Write the subtraction sentence shown by the pictures.

1.  _____

2. 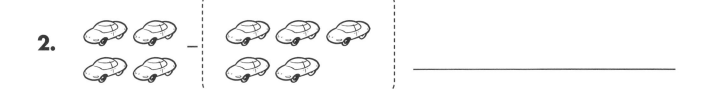 _____

3. 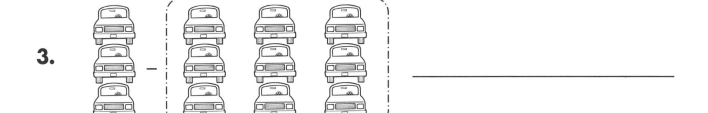 _____

4. _____

DO MORE

Read each subtraction sentence aloud.

0-7424-2881-8 *Using the Standards—Algebra*

Name _____ Date _____

Target Addition

Directions: Color the sections of the target below that make a true addition sentence. Write the number sentences.

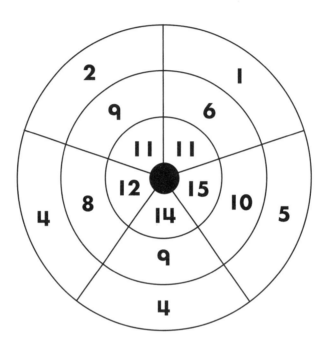

_____   _____

_____

DO MORE

Make a target where the bullseye adds up to 21.

Name _____ Date _____

Target Subtraction

Directions: Color the sections of the target below that make a true subtraction sentence. Write the number sentence.

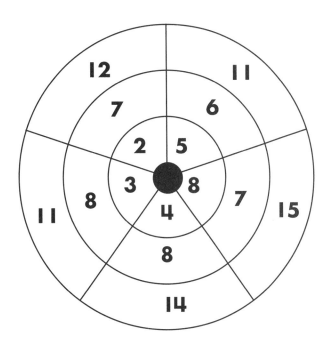

_____ _____

_____

THINK

How can you use a target to make a magic circle puzzle?

0-7424-2881-8 *Using the Standards—Algebra*

Name _____ Date _____

Sum Search

Directions: Work with a partner. Use two different colors of counters. Use the counters to model each addition expression. Match each addition expression with the correct sum. You may use a sum more than once.

1. $8 + 3 =$

2. $4 + 6 =$

3. $6 + 5 =$

4. $3 + 3 =$

5. $5 + 4 =$

6. $8 + 1 =$

7. $6 + 6 =$

8. $4 + 3 =$

9. $2 + 6 =$

10. $3 + 2 =$

| 10 |
| 5 |
| 9 |
| 8 |
| 12 |
| 6 |
| 3 |
| 1 |
| 11 |
| 2 |
| 4 |
| 7 |

DO MORE

Make up addition expressions to match the sums you did not use. How do you know your expression matches the sum?

Published by Instructional Fair. Copyright protected.

0-7424-2881-8 *Using the Standards—Algebra*

Name _____ Date _____

Difference Search

Directions: Work with a partner. Use two different colors of counters. Use the counters to model each subtraction expression. Match each subtraction expression with the correct difference. You may use a difference more than once.

1. $11 - 3 =$

2. $9 - 9 =$

3. $5 - 3 =$

4. $7 - 4 =$

5. $12 - 2 =$

6. $11 - 6 =$

7. $12 - 1 =$

8. $10 - 7 =$

9. $8 - 3 =$

10. $6 - 0 =$

| 10 |
| 5 |
| 9 |
| 8 |
| 0 |
| 6 |
| 3 |
| 1 |
| 11 |
| 2 |
| 4 |
| 7 |

DO MORE

Make up subtraction expressions to match the differences you did not use. How do you know your expression matches the difference?

0-7424-2881-8 *Using the Standards—Algebra*

Name _____ Date _____

Horsing Around

Directions: Tony Pony is playing Hide-and-Seek with his friends. He knows they hide in the barn that has a sum of 10 and a difference of 3. Use counters to model each number sentence. Where are Tony's friends hiding?

1
2 + 3 =
9 − 3 =

2
7 + 4 =
5 − 3 =

3
4 + 4 =
7 − 3 =

4
6 + 2 =
9 − 6 =

5
9 + 3 =
10 − 4 =

6
3 + 7 =
8 − 5 =

7
3 + 5 =
12 − 6 =

8
6 + 5 =
9 − 7 =

9
4 + 3 =
11 − 9 =

DO MORE

Color the barns that have a sum of 8 blue. Color the barns that have a difference of 2 red. Tell how you decided which barns to color.

76

0-7424-2881-8 *Using the Standards—Algebra*

Name _____ Date _____

Follow the Clues

Directions: Use counters to find the sum or difference of each square. Read each clue. Follow the directions. Cross out the squares that will not work. Color the secret square.

1. The secret square does not have a difference of 2.
2. The secret square does not have a sum of 9.
3. The secret square does not have a 7 in the expression.
4. The secret square does not have a difference of 1.
5. The secret square does not have a sum or difference of 4.
6. The secret square does not have a sum or difference of 8.
7. The secret square has the greatest sum remaining.

7 + 3	12 – 4	5 – 4	9 + 2
8 – 4	6 + 3	4 – 2	2 – 0
0 + 4	8 – 1	2 + 8	10 – 7
6 – 5	3 + 4	3 + 5	11 – 6

THINK

How do you know the square you chose is the secret square? Explain your thinking to your class.

0-7424-2881-8 *Using the Standards—Algebra*

Name _____ Date _____

Family Matters

Directions: Use counters to find each sum and difference. Match a number sentence from column A and a number sentence from column B that use the same numbers. (The numbers may be in a different order.)

1. | 8 + 3 =   2 + 5 =

2. | 5 + 2 =   12 – 5 =

3. | 7 + 5 =   3 + 8 =

4. | 3 + 6 =   10 – 3 =

5. | 6 + 2 =   8 – 6 =

6. | 3 + 7 =   6 + 3 =

DO MORE

Work with a friend. Write two more addition or subtraction sentences for each fact family.

0-7424-2881-8 *Using the Standards—Algebra*

Name _____ Date _____

What Would You Do?

Directions: Read each story. Circle **add** or **subtract** to tell how you would solve the problem.

1. Some bears are sleeping in a motel. More bears come in to the motel. How many bears are there in all?

   add   **subtract**

2. Some butterflies go to the bowling alley. Some butterflies go to the car wash. How many more butterflies go to the car wash than go to the bowling alley?

   add   **subtract**

3. Some bees went on a picnic in the park. Some bees went skateboarding in the park. How many bees were in the park altogether?

   add   **subtract**

4. Some penguins like to eat tacos for lunch. Some penguins like to eat spaghetti for lunch. How many more penguins like tacos than like spaghetti?

   add   **subtract**

THINK

Which words in each problem helped you decide to add or to subtract? Make a list of these words and compare lists with a friend.

0-7424-2881-8 *Using the Standards—Algebra*

It's Your Choice

Directions: Listen to the story. Circle **addition** or **subtraction** to tell what
you would do to solve the problem. Write a number sentence
to solve the problem.

1. Five cars went to see the new gas station
being built. Six other cars came, too.
How many cars in all went to watch?

addition   **subtraction**   _____

2. Eight cows like chocolate milk. Three cows
like white milk. How many more cows
like chocolate milk than white milk?

addition   **subtraction**   _____

3. Ten cats were napping in the sun. Four
cats decided to go play with some yarn.
How many cats were left napping?

addition   **subtraction**   _____

4. Six seals went to the movies. Two seals
bought popcorn to eat during the movie.
How many seals did not buy popcorn?

addition   **subtraction**   _____

80

It's Your Choice (cont.)

5. Tillie Turtle baked 12 cupcakes for a party. Tillie ate 6 of the cupcakes before she got to the party. How many cupcakes were left?

    addition   **subtraction**   _____

6. Mazie Mammoth bought 8 bracelets to wear on her tusks. Three of the bracelets fell off when she took a bath. How many bracelets does Mazie have left?

    addition   **subtraction**   _____

7. Seven bunnies were in the store trying on bathing suits. Four more bunnies were in the store trying on T-shirts. How many bunnies were in the store altogether?

    addition   **subtraction**   _____

8. Mr. Mouse sent 5 e-mails this morning and 7 e-mails this afternoon. How many e-mails did he send in all?

    addition   **subtraction**   _____

DO MORE

Make up an addition story and a subtraction story of your own. Tell your stories to the class and have them write a number sentence to solve the problem.

81

0-7424-2881-8 *Using the Standards—Algebra*

Name _____ Date _____

Create Your Own Problems

Directions: Make up your own addition and subtraction problems.

Addition

_____

_____

Subtraction

_____

_____

0-7424-2881-8 *Using the Standards—Algebra*

Name _____ Date _____

Check Your Skills

1. Write the addition or subtraction sentence shown by the pictures.

_____

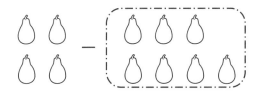

_____

2. Match the number sentences that use the same numbers.

3 + 6 = 9	2 + 8 = 10
10 − 2 = 8	7 + 2 = 9
5 + 1 = 6	9 − 3 = 6
9 − 7 = 2	10 − 4 = 6
10 − 6 = 4	1 + 5 = 6

3. Write an addition or subtraction sentence to solve the problem.

Twelve owls flew at night. Three owls
bumped into a tree and stopped flying.
How many owls were still flying?   _____

Six squirrels had a party. Five more
squirrels came to the party. How many
squirrels were at the party altogether?   _____

83

Published by Instructional Fair. Copyright protected.   0-7424-2881-8 *Using the Standards—Algebra*

Name _____ Date _____

Something's Different

Directions: Look at the two pictures below. Can you find all the changes? Circle the things that have changed.

DO MORE

Tell a friend how each thing has changed.

0-7424-2881-8 *Using the Standards—Algebra*

Name _____ Date _____

Not Quite the Same

Directions: Look at the flower at the left. Then, look at the flower on the right. Tell how each flower has changed.

left   **right**

1.

_____

2.

_____

3.

_____

4.

_____

DO MORE

Find something at home that has changed. Draw a picture of how it used to be and how it is now. Show your picture to the class and tell how it has changed.

0-7424-2881-8 *Using the Standards—Algebra*

What Might Happen If...

Directions: Draw the objects to show how they might change.

What might happen if these things got taller?

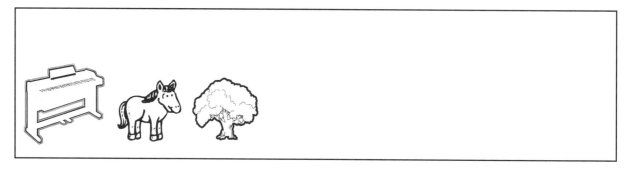

What might happen if these things got shorter?

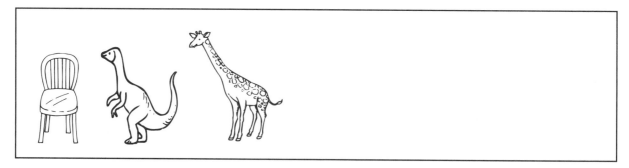

What might happen if these things got wider?

THINK

Which of these changes might really happen? Which could not happen?

     0-7424-2881-8 *Using the Standards—Algebra*

Name _____ Date _____

A Change of Direction

Directions: There are 5 birds in the neighborhood. They fly from tree to tree. Follow the directions to find where each bird flies to next. Mark an X on the correct square.

1. The first bird flew two squares right and one square down.
2. The second bird flew three squares right.
3. The third bird flew one square up and three squares right.
4. The fourth bird flew two squares down and three squares left.
5. The fifth bird flew one square right and one square up.

left   right

DO MORE

Draw another bird. Tell a friend how this bird flew. Have your friend draw the bird where it landed.

0-7424-2881-8 *Using the Standards—Algebra*

Name _____ Date _____

Monster Changes

Directions: Draw the monster. Change three things about the monster in your drawing. You can make it shorter or taller, change its clothes, or change its color. You can think of your own changes, too. Show your monster to the class. Explain what changes you made to the monster.

DO MORE

Draw 2 monsters. Change 3 things about the first monster to make the second monster. Ask a friend to find the changes.

0-7424-2881-8 *Using the Standards—Algebra*

Name _____ Date _____

Then and Now

Directions: Look at the pictures. Circle the things that have changed.

DO MORE

Describe how each thing you circled has changed.

0-7424-2881-8 *Using the Standards—Algebra*

Name _____ Date _____

The Dog Ate My Homework

Directions: The dog ate my homework, so I had to do it again. Look at what I drew the first time and compare it to what I drew the second time. Tell what has changed.

1. ☐

2. 18

3. ✏

4. ⊖

5. yes

6. red

7. $3 + 4 = 7$

8. 9

1. ☐

2. 17

3. ✏

4. ⊕

5. yes

6. blue

7. $4 + 3 = 7$

8. 9

DO MORE

Find 3 things in your classroom that have changed in the past few days. Draw a picture of how they used to look and how they look now. Explain the changes to the class.

0-7424-2881-8 *Using the Standards—Algebra*

Name _____ Date _____

Chances Are...

Directions: Think about what happens in the real world. Each of these things will change. Circle the picture that shows what is most likely to happen.

I.

Flower gets no water

2.

Drink some water

3.

Candle burns

4.

Takes a bath

THINK

What changes happen to you every day? Make a list and compare it with a friend.

0-7424-2881-8 *Using the Standards—Algebra*

Name _____ Date _____

Seasonal Changes

Directions: As the seasons change, what we need to wear can change, too. Draw clothes on the pig to show how clothing would change for each season.

Spring

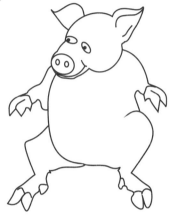

Summer

Fall

Winter

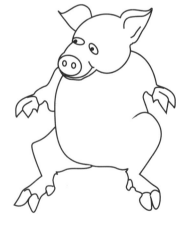

DO MORE

Draw 4 pictures of what you would wear in each season. Show your drawings to the class and explain why you chose the clothes you did.

92

Name _____ Date _____

Calendar Changes

Directions: The same dates in a month do not always fall on the same days of the week. Look at these calendars.

SUNDAY	MONDAY	TUESDAY	WEDNESDAY	THURSDAY	FRIDAY	SATURDAY
1	2	3	4	5	6	7
8	9	10	11	12	13	14
15	16	17	18	19	20	21
22	23	24	25	26	27	28
29	30	31				

SUNDAY	MONDAY	TUESDAY	WEDNESDAY	THURSDAY	FRIDAY	SATURDAY
			1	2	3	4
5	6	7	8	9	10	11
12	13	14	15	16	17	18
19	20	21	22	23	24	25
26	27	28	29	30		

SUNDAY	MONDAY	TUESDAY	WEDNESDAY	THURSDAY	FRIDAY	SATURDAY
					1	2
3	4	5	6	7	8	9
10	11	12	13	14	15	16
17	18	19	20	21	22	23
24	25	26	27	28	29	30
31						

0-7424-2881-8 *Using the Standards—Algebra*

Name _____ Date _____

Calendar Changes (cont.)

Directions: Use the calendars on page 93 to find the changes.

1. What days are the 5th of each month? _____

   _____

   _____

2. The second Tuesday of each month has what date? _____

   _____

   _____

3. What days are the 25th of each month? _____

   _____

   _____

4. What days are the 10th of each month? _____

   _____

   _____

5. The fourth Thursday of each month has what date?

   _____

   _____

   _____

DO MORE

Find the date of your birthday on each calendar. On which days would you celebrate your birthday?

0-7424-2881-8 *Using the Standards—Algebra*

Name _____ Date _____

Paper Clip Differences

Directions: Next to each length, write the number of small paper clips that fit on the line. Then write a math sentence in the box that shows the difference between the two lengths.

1. ├──────────────────────────┤

├──────────┤

2. ├─────────────────┤

├──────────┤

3. ├────────────────────────────────┤

├──────────────┤

THINK

Would it be easy to measure things using only paper clips? Why or why not?

0-7424-2881-8 *Using the Standards—Algebra*

Name _____ Date _____

How Much Taller?

Directions: Use cubes to measure each plant.
Tell how much each plant has grown.

1. Plant A = _____

Plant B = _____

Difference = _____

2. Plant A = _____

Plant B = _____

Difference = _____

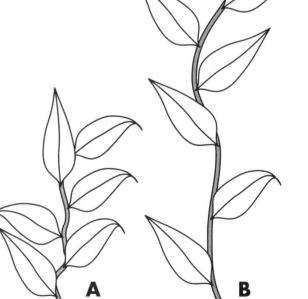

A   B   A   B

DO MORE

Find the difference between the small plant on the left and the large plant on the right. Explain to a friend how you measure each plant and how you found the difference.

0-7424-2881-8 *Using the Standards—Algebra*

Name _____ Date _____

Bonita Grows Up

Directions: Every year, Bonita's doctor measures her to see how much she has grown. This chart shows what Bonita measured each year.

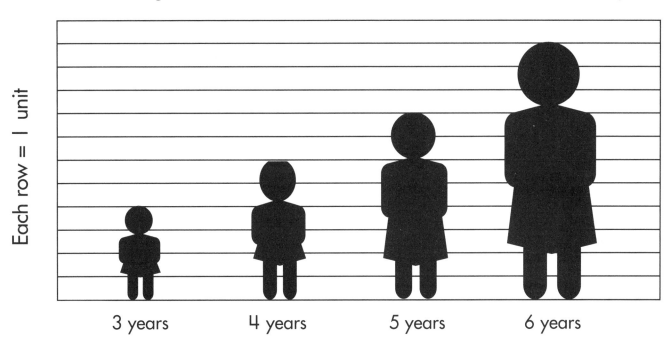

Each row = 1 unit

3 years   4 years   5 years   6 years

1. How many units did Bonita grow between 3 and 4 years old? _____

2. How many units did she grow between 4 and 6 years old? _____

3. How many units did she grow between 3 and 5 years old? _____

4. How many units did Bonita grow between 3 and 6 years old? _____

DO MORE

Work with a partner. Measure yourself and your partner. Who is taller? How much taller?

0-7424-2881-8 *Using the Standards—Algebra*

Name _____ Date _____

How Did It Change?

Directions: Read each change and color the number that shows how that change happened. Use cubes to help.

1. I used to have 5, but now I have 8. How did it change?

| + 3 | + 2 | − 3 |

2. I used to have 12, but now I have 6. How did it change?

| − 7 | + 6 | − 6 |

3. I used to have 4, but now I have 9. How did it change?

| + 5 | − 5 | + 3 |

4. I used to have 2, but now I have 7. How did it change?

| − 5 | + 4 | + 5 |

5. I used to have 10, but now I have 6. How did it change?

| + 4 | − 4 | + 3 |

DO MORE

Make up your own clues for two changes. Have a friend tell how the numbers changed.

0-7424-2881-8 *Using the Standards—Algebra*

Name _____ Date _____

I Used to Be...

Directions: Each circle started on a different number. Find the number each circle started on by reading the clues.

1.

> I used to be on the number that is 4 more than this number.

1	2	3	4	😊	6	7	8	9	10
11	12	13	14	15	16	17	18	19	20

What was the starting number? _____

2.

> I used to be on the number that is 5 less than this number.

1	2	3	4	5	6	7	8	9	10
11	12	13	14	15	16	😊	18	19	20

What was the starting number? _____

3.

> I used to be on the number that is 7 less than this number.

1	2	3	4	5	6	7	8	9	10
😊	12	13	14	15	16	17	18	19	20

What was the starting number? _____

THINK

How did you know how to find the starting number?
Explain your thinking to a friend.

99

Name _____ Date _____

Get Them All!

Directions: Use the cards on pages 121–128.

Place the Number Cards and Change Cards on the correct square. Take turns. Take a Number Card and a Change Card. Change the number on your Number Card by the rule on the Change Card. Use a counter to cover each number you make. The first to get all the numbers wins.

1
2
3
4
5
6
7
8
9
10
11
12

Number Cards

Change Cards

12
11
10
9
8
7
6
5
4
3
2
1

0-7424-2881-8 *Using the Standards—Algebra*

Name _____ Date _____

A Change in Quantity

Directions: The pictures show a group of objects before something
changed and after something changed. Write a number
sentence to show how they changed.

1.

2.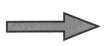

3.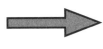

4.

0-7424-2881-8 *Using the Standards—Algebra*

Name _____ Date _____

A Change in Quantity (cont.)

5.

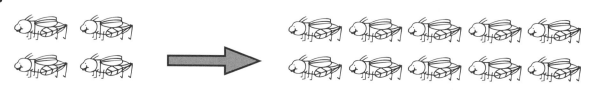

6.

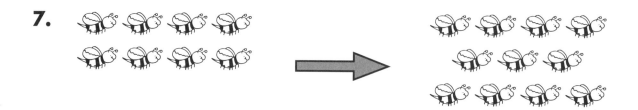

7.

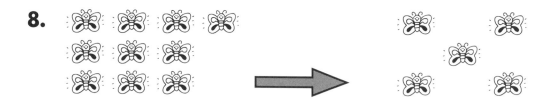

8.

THINK

Can every change be described by a number sentence?
Explain your answer.

0-7424-2881-8 *Using the Standards—Algebra*

Name _____ Date _____

Up or Down?

Directions: These numbers have changed. Find each change by adding and subtracting.

1.

Change by 3

7

Add _____

Subtract _____

2.

Change by 1

4

Add _____

Subtract _____

3.

Change by 4

6

Add _____

Subtract _____

4.

Change by 5

8

Add _____

Subtract _____

0-7424-2881-8 *Using the Standards—Algebra*

Name _____ Date _____

Up or Down? (cont.)

5.

10 [Change by 2]

Add _____

Subtract _____

6.

5 [Change by 3]

Add _____

Subtract _____

7.

3 [Change by 0]

Add _____

Subtract _____

8.

9 [Change by 4]

Add _____

Subtract _____

9.

11 [Change by 5]

Add _____

Subtract _____

DO MORE

Make up your own numbers and changes. Challenge your class to find two ways your number could have changed.

0-7424-2881-8 *Using the Standards—Algebra*

Name _____ Date _____

Stories About Change

Directions: Listen to each funny story about change. Write an addition or subtraction sentence to solve each problem.

1. The princess keeps her 8 rubies in her closet. She found 3 more rubies in her left shoe. How many rubies does she have now?

_____

2. Last year Oscar Otter won 6 trophies for playing baseball. This year Oscar won 3 more trophies. How many trophies does he have now?

_____

3. Bessie the Cow had 7 fancy dresses. The dry cleaners ruined 2 of the dresses. How many dresses does Bessie have now?

_____

4. Pealer the Dalmatian used to have 12 spots, but his mother scrubbed him too hard in the bath and washed off 5 spots. How many spots does he have now?

_____

0-7424-2881-8 *Using the Standards—Algebra*

Name _____ Date _____

Stories About Change (cont.)

5. Buster Bee used to run into 3 stop signs on his way to the rose garden. Somebody put up 5 more stop signs. How many stop signs are there now?

_____

6. Eloise Elephant used to weigh 9 tons. She went on a diet and lost 6 tons. How many tons does Eloise weigh now?

_____

7. Pierre Penguin used to have 2 copies of his driver's license. He made one more copy to keep in his wallet. How many copies does he have now?

_____

8. Grom the Caveman had 7 wheels on his skateboard until he ran into a boulder. The boulder knocked off 5 wheels. How many wheels are on the skateboard now?

_____

DO MORE

Make up an addition change story and a subtraction change story. Tell the stories to your class and have them solve the problems.

0-7424-2881-8 *Using the Standards—Algebra*

Name _____ Date _____

Create Your Own Problems

Directions: Make up your own problems about change.

Use the spaces to show how something changes over time. Have a friend tell what has changed.

Use the space to show how a group of objects changes. Draw the pictures. Have a friend write an addition or subtraction sentence to show the change.

0-7424-2881-8 *Using the Standards—Algebra*

Name _____   Date _____

Check Your Skills

1. Circle the things that have changed.

2. Find where each circle started.

> I used to be on the number that is 8 more than this number.

1	2	3	☺	5	6	7	8	9	10
11	12	13	14	15	16	17	18	19	20

What was the starting number? _____

> I used to be on the number that is 5 less than this number.

1	2	3	4	5	6	7	8	9	10
11	☺	13	14	15	16	17	18	19	20

What was the starting number? _____

3. Find the change by addition and subtraction.

> Change by 4

8

Add _____

Subtract _____

0-7424-2881-8 *Using the Standards—Algebra*

Posttest

1. Find the pattern. Draw the next three shapes in the pattern.

2. Find the pattern. Make the same pattern using colors.

4   6   6   7   4   6   6   7   4   6   6   7

3. Write + or − to make each number sentence true.

a. 9 ◯ 2 = 11

b. 5 ◯ 0 = 5

c. 3 ◯ 8 = 11

d. 9 ◯ 3 = 12

e. 10 ◯ 3 = 7

f. 8 ◯ 5 = 3

4. Write >, <, or =.

a. 8 ◯ 6

b. 10 ◯ 11

c. 5 ◯ 5

d. 7 ◯ 7

e. 11 ◯ 9

f. 4 ◯ 5

0-7424-2881-8 *Using the Standards—Algebra*

Posttest (cont.)

5. Write an addition or subtraction sentence to solve each problem.

    a. Milton Mallard found 7 golf balls in the lake. He found 3 more under a bush. How many golf balls did he find in all? _____

    b. Nine polar bears went snowboarding. Two bears had their own snowboards. How many bears had to rent snowboards? _____

6. Circle the things that have changed.

7. Read the clues and circle the mystery numbers.

    a. I am > 5. I am < 10. What numbers could I be?

1	2	3	4	5	6	7	8	9	10	11	12	13	14	15

    b. I am > 8. I am < 12. What numbers could I be?

1	2	3	4	5	6	7	8	9	10	11	12	13	14	15

0-7424-2881-8 *Using the Standards—Algebra*

Answer Key

1. The next shapes are circle, circle, square.
2. Sample colors: blue, blue, red, green.
3. **a.** −   **d.** −
   b. +   **e.** +
   c. −   **f.** +
4. **a.** <   **d.** >
   b. =   **e.** >
   c. <   **f.** =
5. **a.** $7 - 4 = 3$
   b. $8 + 2 = 10$
   c. $2 + 5 = 7$
6. The hair and the tears have changed.
7. **a.** 4 or 5
   b. 10, 11, 12, or 13

1. The shapes are all triangles. They all have three corners. Each group has small, medium, and large shapes. Students should draw two triangles, differing in size.
2. The shapes are all squares. They all have four corners. Each group has small, medium, and large shapes. Students should draw two squares, differing in size.
3. The shapes are all pentagons. They all have five corners. Each group has small, medium, and large shapes. Students should draw two pentagons, differing in size.

Students should circle 2 squares and 2 rectangles. Check students' sorting by color. The shapes could also be sorted by size: big and small.

Students can sort by shape (star, heart, diamond, moon), by size (small, medium, large), or by pattern.

"My heart" is the large heart to the right in the middle of the page.

1. 4 mittens
2. 6 mittens
3. 3 mittens
4. 5 mittens
5. 7 mittens

Check students' work to see that all outfits match.

There are 5 matching pairs of flowers.

yellow

blue

0-7424-2881-8 *Using the Standards—Algebra*

Answer Key (cont.)

A Sunny Day in Beartown **17**

Yummy, Yummy **18**

The soup may or may not be crossed out.

Button Up! **19**
1. 1, 3, 2
2. 3, 1, 2
3. 2, 1, 3

Read Any Good Books Lately? **20**

(From top to bottom)
1. 1, 4, 5, 2, 3
2. 3, 2, 5, 4, 1

Scrambled Stories **21**

Answers will vary.

New Girl in Town **22**
a. 3
b. 4
c. 1
d. 2

One, Two, Three. **23**

Numbers colored are 3, 6, 9, 12, 15, 18, 21, 24, 27, 30, 33, 36, 39, 42, 45, and 48. They show a diagonal pattern. The dots connect to reveal a hippopotamus.

Again and Again and Again **24**
1. triangle
2. square
3. circle
4. star

Lions and Tigers and Bears **25**
1. bear
2. pig
3. frog
4. seal

0-7424-2881-8 *Using the Standards—Algebra*

What's Missing Here? 26
   1. orange
   2. pear
   3. watermelon
   4. apple
   5. watermelon
The next 3 objects would be:
   1. grape, orange, orange
   2. apple, pear, orange
   3. apple, banana, watermelon
   4. apple, pumpkin, pumpkin
   5. watermelon, banana, apple

Pattern Synonyms 27
   1. Check students' patterns.
   2. Have students explain how the two patterns are the same.

Little Red Riding Hood's Hoods 28
Last three patterns are:

Unlock the Door 29
   1. Door 1223
   2. Door 2123
   3. Door 1132
   4. Door 3312
   5. Door 1321

Covering Patterns. 30
Check drawings and coloring patterns.

Pretend Patterns 31
   1. 8 3 8 9
   2. no pattern
   3. H J K P
   4. daisy, rose, rose, daisy
   5. no pattern

Simon Says 32
   1. Check number charts. Circled numbers are:
   2. 19
   3. 31
   4. 29
   5. 13
   6. 48
   7. 36
   8. 23

Copy Cat 33
   1.
   2. 5 7 0 7 5 7 0 7 5 7 0

   3. 9 9 3 5 9 9 3 5 9 9 3

   4. S P H T S P H T S P

   5.

Patterns 1 and 3 are alike; patterns 2 and 5 are alike.

Growing Up 34
   1.
   2.
   3.

Can I Have Your Number? 35
   1. 5 3 3 3 3
   2. 8 8 8 1 1 1
   3. 7 4 4 4 7

The Same, But Different 36
Check patterns.

0-7424-2881-8 *Using the Standards—Algebra*

Answer Key (cont.)

Petal Patterns 37

Growing Shapes 38
1. 4 squares in all
2. 9 squares in all
3. 16 squares in all
4. 25 squares in all
    Help students see that the sides grow by 1, and the total squares grows in a pattern of add 5, add 7, add 9....

A Real Fashion Statement 39
Check color patterns.

Secret Code 40–41
Check to see that the letters are numbered consecutively from 1 to 26.
    Question: What clothes does a house wear?
    Answer: Address.

Half Again 42

How Does Your Garden Grow? 43
1. G
2. R
3. G
4. G
5. R

Create Your Own Problems 44
Answers may vary.

Check Your Skills 45
1.
2. From left to right: 1, 4, 2, 3
3. 1 5 3 and O F F
4. The next shapes are circle, square, square, triangle, circle.

Equal Rights–and Lefts 46
1. Draw 3 blocks on the right; both sides have 4 blocks.
2. Draw 3 blocks on the left; both sides have 5 blocks.
3. Draw 5 blocks on the left; both sides have 8 blocks.

0-7424-2881-8 *Using the Standards—Algebra*

Answer Key (cont.)

Make It Equal 47
Groupings may vary.

Button, Button 48
1. less
2. more
3. more
4. less

More Than One Answer 49
1. Accept any number 1–6.
2. Accept any number 6 or greater.
3. Accept any number 1–8.
4. Accept any number 9 or greater.

Solve the Mystery 50
1. 5, 6
2. 9, 10, 11, 12
3. 2, 3, 4, 5
4. 7, 8, 9, 10, 11, 12, 13

Thanks for Nothing! 51
1. 5; draw 5 dimes
2. 9; draw 9 dimes
3. 7; draw 7 dimes
4. 4; draw 4 dimes

What's the Story? 52
1. subtract
2. add
3. subtract
4. add
5. subtract

Touchdown! 53
Monitor students as they play.

You Be the Teacher 54
1. Draw one more square.
2. OK
3. Cross out one heart.
4. Cross out one triangle.

It's Puzzling 55
1. d
2. h
3. f
4. a
5. c
6. g
7. b
8. e

Oops! 56
1. 5
2. 8
3. 5
4. 4
5. 7

Mixed Signals 57
1. <
2. >
3. >
4. <
5. =
6. <

Signs of the Times 58
1. +
2. +
3. −
4. −
5. +

 0-7424-2881-8 *Using the Standards—Algebra*

Answer Key (cont.)

Do It Yourself 59

Check children's symbols for consistency of use. Exercises 1 and 4 show subtraction; exercises 2, 3, and 5 show addition.

A Rose By Any Other Name 60

Answers will vary. Examples are given.

1. $3 + 4, 9 - 2$
2. $6 + 6, 3 + 9$
3. $1 + 5, 9 - 3$
4. $4 + 6, 12 - 2$
5. $1 + 2, 5 - 2$
6. $4 + 4, 11 - 3$
7. $12 - 1, 5 + 6$
8. $5 + 4, 10 - 1$
9. $2 + 2, 7 - 3$
10. $1 + 1, 6 - 4$

Treasure Hunt 61

It's a Jungle Out There. 62

There are 2 elephants, 5 lions, and 3 monkeys. Check graphs.

Reading Pictures 63

1. 6
2. 7
3. 9
4. 13
5. 4

Best Graph, Bar None 64

There are 5 fish, 4 dogs, and 6 cats.

Communicating 65

1. 7
2. 5
3. 7
4. 12
5. 3

A New Way to Count. 66

There are 9 turtles, 5 dolphins, and 7 owls.

Reading the Handwriting. 67

1. 8
2. 5
3. 20
4. 5
5. 15

Create Your Own Problems 68

Answers will vary.

Check Your Skills 69

1. The right side should show 6 blocks in any arrangement.
2. a. +   c. −
   b. −   d. +
3. a. >   c. <
   b. =   d. >
4. a. 9, 10, 11, or 12
   b. 3, 4, 5, or 6

0-7424-2881-8 *Using the Standards—Algebra*

Answer Key (cont.)

  1. $5 + 2 = 7$
  2. $3 + 8 = 11$
  3. $6 + 3 = 9$
  4. $5 + 3 = 8$

  1. $10 - 4 = 6$
  2. $9 - 5 = 4$
  3. $12 - 9 = 3$
  4. $10 - 5 = 5$

$2 + 9 = 11$
$4 + 8 = 12$
$5 + 10 = 15$

$11 - 6 = 5$
$15 - 7 = 8$
$11 - 8 = 3$

  1. 11
  2. 10
  3. 11
  4. 6
  5. 9
  6. 9
  7. 12
  8. 7
  9. 8
  10. 5

  1. 8
  2. 0
  3. 2
  4. 3
  5. 10
  6. 5
  7. 11
  8. 3
  9. 5
  10. 6

Tony's friends are hiding in barn 6.

The secret square is in the upper right corner:
$9 + 2$.

1. $8 + 3 = 11$ ⟶ $3 + 8 = 11$
2. $5 + 2 = 7$ ⟶ $2 + 5 = 7$
3. $7 + 5 = 12$ ⟶ $12 - 5 = 7$
4. $3 + 6 = 9$ ⟶ $6 + 3 = 9$
5. $6 + 2 = 8$ ⟶ $8 - 6 = 2$
6. $3 + 7 = 10$ ⟶ $10 - 3 = 7$

  1. add
  2. subtract
  3. add
  4. subtract

     0-7424-2881-8 *Using the Standards—Algebra*

Answer Key (cont.)

It's Your Choice 80–81
1. addition; 5 + 6 = 11
2. subtraction; 8 – 3 = 5
3. subtraction; 10 – 4 = 6
4. subtraction; 6 – 2 = 4
5. subtraction; 12 – 6 = 6
6. subtraction; 8 – 3 = 5
7. addition; 7 + 4 = 11
8. addition; 5 + 7 = 12

Create Your Own Problems 82
Answers will vary.

Check Your Skills 83
1. 7 + 5 = 12; 11 – 7 = 4
2.

3 + 6 = 9	2 + 8 = 10
10 – 2 = 8	7 + 2 = 9
5 + 1 = 6	9 – 3 = 6
9 – 7 = 2	10 – 4 = 6
10 – 6 = 4	1 + 5 = 6

(3 + 6 = 9 → 7 + 2 = 9; 10 – 2 = 8 → 9 – 3 = 6; 5 + 1 = 6 → 10 – 4 = 6; 9 – 7 = 2 → 2 + 8 = 10; 10 – 6 = 4 → 1 + 5 = 6)

3. 12 – 3 = 9; 6 + 5 = 11

Something's Different 84
There are now two birds instead of one. The woman on the bike is no longer pulling a baby. The picnic basket is now a trunk. There are 2 girls and a boy playing with the flying disc instead of two boys and a girl. There are now two fawns instead of one.

Not Quite the Same 85
1. The flower is bigger.
2. The flower is smaller.
3. The flower is shorter.
4. The flower is taller.

What Would Happen If.... 86
Check drawings.

A Change of Direction 87

1 (runner)					
	2 (runner)	1		2	
			3		
3 (runner)			4 (runner)		
					5
4				5 (runner)	

Monster Changes 88
Check drawings.

Then and Now 89
The duck, horse, giraffe, and cake have changed. The duck and horse have grown larger; the giraffe has grown taller; the cake became a piece of pie.

The Dog Ate My Homework 90
1. The shape was a square, but now it's a rectangle.
2. The number was 18, but now it is 17.
3. The pencil was short, but now it is longer.
4. The circle showed halves, but now it shows quarters.
5. No change
6. The color was red, but now it is blue.
7. The addends were 3 + 4, but now they are 4 + 3 (in a different order).
8. No change

Published by Instructional Fair. Copyright protected.

0-7424-2881-8 *Using the Standards—Algebra*

Answer Key (cont.)

Chances Are... . . . . **91**
1. the droopy flower
2. the glass with less water
3. the shorter candle
4. the clean child

Seasonal Changes **92**
Check drawings. Accept reasonable clothes for your region.

Calendar Changes **93–94**
1. Thursday, Sunday, Tuesday
2. 10th, 14th, 12th
3. Wednesday, Saturday, Monday
4. Tuesday, Friday, Sunday
5. 26th, 23rd, 28th

Paper Clip Differences **95**
1. $4 - 2 = 2$
2. $3 - 2 = 1$
3. $5 - 3 = 2$

How Much Taller? **96**
Plant heights and differences will vary depending on the types of cubes used.

Bonita Grows Up **97**
1. 2 units
2. 5 units
3. 4 units
4. 7 units
Monitor measurement activities.

How Did It Change? **98**
1. $+ 3$
2. $- 6$
3. $+ 5$
4. $+ 5$
5. $- 4$

I Used to Be... . . . . **99**
1. 9
2. 12
3. 4

Get Them All! **100**
Monitor play.

A Change in Quantity **101–102**
1. $5 - 2 = 3$
2. $7 - 5 = 2$
3. $3 + 3 = 6$
4. $2 + 6 = 8$
5. $4 + 6 = 10$
6. $9 - 4 = 5$
7. $8 + 3 = 11$
8. $10 - 5 = 5$

Up or Down? **103–104**
1. $7 + 3 = 10; 7 - 3 = 4$
2. $4 + 1 = 5; 4 - 1 = 3$
3. $6 + 4 = 10; 6 - 4 = 2$
4. $8 + 5 = 13; 8 - 5 = 3$
5. $10 + 2 = 12; 10 - 2 = 8$
6. $5 + 3 = 8; 5 - 3 = 2$
7. $3 + 0 = 3; 3 - 0 = 3$
8. $9 + 4 = 13; 9 - 4 = 5$
9. $11 + 5 = 16; 11 - 5 = 6$

Stories About Change **105–106**
1. $8 + 3 = 11$
2. $6 + 3 = 9$
3. $7 - 2 = 5$
4. $12 - 5 = 7$
5. $3 + 5 = 8$
6. $9 - 6 = 3$
7. $2 + 1 = 3$
8. $7 - 5 = 2$

      0-7424-2881-8 *Using the Standards—Algebra*

Answer Key (cont.)

Create Your Own Problems 107

Answers will vary.

Check Your Skills 108

1. The girl has a bow in her hair and is smiling in the first picture.
2. 12, 7
3. 8 + 4 = 12; 8 – 4 = 4

Posttest 109–110

1. The next shapes are square, circle, triangle.
2. Sample colors: blue, red, red, green
3. **a.** –   **d.** +
   b. + or –   **e.** –
   c. +   **f.** –
4. **a.** >   **d.** =
   b. <   **e.** >
   c. =   **f.** <
5. **a.** 7 + 3 = 10
   b. 9 – 2 = 7
6. The horns, smile, spots, and tail have changed.
7. **a.** 6, 7, 8, or 9
   b. 9, 10, or 11

1

2

3

4

5

6

0-7424-2881-8 *Using the Standards—Algebra*

Number Card

Number Card

Number Card

Number Card

Number Card

Number Card

7

8

9

10

11

12

0-7424-2881-8 *Using the Standards—Algebra*

Number Card

Number Card

Number Card

Number Card

Number Card

Number Card

0-7424-2881-8 *Using the Standards—Algebra*

Lose a Turn	**Take Another Turn**
Free 5	**Free 12**
Change by 1	**Change by 2**

0-7424-2881-8 *Using the Standards—Algebra*

Number Card

Number Card

Number Card

Number Card

Change Card

Change Card

0-7424-2881-8 *Using the Standards—Algebra*

Change by 3

Change by 4

Change by 1

Change by 2

Change by 3

Change by 4

0-7424-2881-8 *Using the Standards—Algebra*

Change Card

Change Card

Change Card

Change Card

Change Card

Change Card

0-7424-2881-8 *Using the Standards—Algebra*